MW00635588

Twelve Bags Fulled

A collection of felted handbags for the whole year through

by
Terry L. Ross
Terry Ross Designs

www.terryrossdesigns.com

Photography by Vicki Bedford

SAN: 852-7113
Terry Ross Designs
481 West Erie Street
Rogers City, MI 49779
989-734-4267

© 2006 Terry L. Ross

ISBN-13: 978-0-9791894-0-1
ISBN-10: 0-9791894-0-3

Photographs
Vicki Bedford

Printed in the USA
First Edition, 2007

For our children, who truly are blessings from the Lord.

Table of Contents

Acknowledgments 2

Introduction 3

Abbreviations, Knitting Terms, and Techniques 5

January -- Starry Nights Party Wristlet 7

February -- Peekaboo Hearts 9

March -- March to Your Own Music 11

April -- Baby Showers 13

May -- May Bouquet 15

June -- Going to the Chapel 19

July -- Watermelon Whimsy 22

August -- Sunny Funflower 24

September -- Back to Work/Back to School Brown Bag 28

October -- Changing Leaves 30

November -- Knitting Together a Family 32

December -- Santa's Got a Brand New Bag 34

Felting Tutorial, Tips, and Tricks 36

Information and Errata 39

About the Designer 41

Acknowledgments

Thank you to my husband Art – for allowing me time and space to express my creativity, and for appreciating it as well.

Thank you to our children Duncan, Abby, and Emma – for letting Mama do "just a few more stitches".

Thank you, Susan Druding – for being a sounding board and brainstorming partner, as well as the Yarn Muse and head cheerleader. Thank you for giving me the impetus to design and the means to achieve it.

Thank you, Crystal Palace Yarns (www.straw.com) – for providing all the gorgeous yarns in these handbags and for encouraging my designing efforts.

Thank you, Denise Daher – for test-knitting for me, giving great feedback and helpful tweaks, and loving my patterns. Thanks for helping me see a way to knit a better watermelon.

Thank you, Vicki Bedford – for giving me the inspiration and a push to knit again after so many years. Your friendship, support, and encouragement over the last many years are priceless, and you are valued far above rubies. Thank you for rekindling my knitting flame and for photographing my bags to show their beauty.

And thank you to women everywhere for having a never-ending love affair with handbags and purses! This book is for you.

Introduction

Technically, there is a difference between felting and fulling, although in the day to day conversations of most knitters, the terms are used interchangeably. In a nutshell, the differences can be summed up in the following way. Felting is a process that creates fabric from raw fibers such as fleece or roving. Fulling is a process which creates fabric from fiber that was first knit or woven into an article of some sort. Regardless of which term you prefer to use, when you practice this wonderful art, you are engaging in an activity that has a long history behind it. It is one of the earliest forms of textile processing in recorded history.

Knitting and other textile arts have had new life breathed into them in recent years as they are rediscovered by those who love to create beauty and enjoy handcrafted clothing, accessories, and homekeeping items. The fiber industry has kept pace by producing more and more varieties of yarns, and the choices available to knitters have increased astronomically. The felting craze has served to fuel that industry even further to produce yarns that are richly colored, patterned, and textured and also suitable for felting. Yarn artisans are producing lovely handpainted yarns and patterns to go with them.

The designs contained in this collection of patterns are great for those who want to become acquainted with this very addictive art, as well as for those who are already seasoned felters and fullers. Each pattern was inspired by a month of the year, and one can easily knit a bag each month of the year, with lots of time to spare. I hope you'll enjoy knitting these bags, but I hope even more that you'll enjoy using them and the tactile pleasure you'll receive from simply touching them.

Thank you for allowing me to bring this collection of handbags to you.

Terry L. Ross

Abbreviations, Knitting Terms and Techniques

BO	Bind off		P2tog	Purl 2 stitches together
CO	Cast On		P3tog	Purl 3 stitches together
dec	Decrease		PM	Place marker
inc	Increase		PSSO	Pass slipped stitch over
K	Knit		PU	Pick up
K2tog	Knit 2 stitches together		ret	Return
K2togTBL	Knit 2 stitches together through the back loop		RH	Right hand
			rnd	Round
K3tog	Knit 3 stitches together		RS	Right side
Kf/b	Knit in the front and back of the same stitch		Sl	Slip
			SSK	Slip, slip, knit
LH	Left hand		SSP	Slip, slip, purl
M1	Make one stitch		st or sts	Stitch or stitches
MC	Main Color		WS	Wrong side
P-wise	Purlwise		YO	Yarn over
P	Purl		YO2	Yarn over 2 times

Garter stitch -- When working flat (back and forth), make garter stitch by knitting all stitches on each row. When working in the round, make garter stitch by knitting one round and then purling one round, repeating the pattern of alternating K and P rounds.

Stockinette stitch -- When working flat (back and forth) make stockinette stitch by knitting on the right side row and purling on the wrong side row. When working in the round, make stockinette stitch by knitting all rounds.

Knitted I-cord -- Cast on the specified number of stitches to a double pointed needle. Without turning, slide the stitches to the right hand end of the same needle. Bring the yarn behind the work from the last cast on stitch and use a second double pointed needle to knit from the first cast on stitch to the end of the row. At the end of each row, slide the stitches back to the right hand end of the needle and knit the next row, always with the yarn in back. The working yarn will tighten the piece into a tube as you knit more rows. Give the tube a tug on the bottom every now and then to encourage the stitches to snug up.

January

Starry Nights Party Wristlet

Materials:

2 balls (100 gr.) Crystal Palace Yarns Fjord in Jet Black (MC)
1 ball (50 gr.) Crystal Palace Yarns Fizz Stardust in Jet Black (Color B)
1 ball (50 gr.) Crystal Palace Yarns Fizz Stardust in White Ice (Color C)
1 ball (50 gr.) Crystal Palace Yarns Squiggle in Jet Black (Color D)
1 ball (50 gr.) Crystal Palace Yarns Deco-Ribbon in Black Silver (Color E)
1 16" US Size 11 (8.0 mm) circular needle
1 set of US Size 11 (8.0 mm) double pointed needles
2 US Size 8 (5.0 mm) double pointed needles
Stitch marker
Tapestry needle
Crochet hook
6 silver-toned ½" metal grommets
Black sewing thread and a sewing needle
1 yard of coordinating ribbon

Dimensions:

Before felting – 13" tall, including picot edge; 7" in diameter, including bottom edge ridge; 6" in diameter, without bottom edge ridge
After felting – 8½" tall, including picot edge; 5½" in diameter, including bottom edge ridge; 4½" in diameter without bottom edge ridge

Bottom of bag:

Using the size 11 double pointed needles and one strand of the MC (or using your favorite method for small diameter circular knitting), CO 8 sts (stitches). All odd numbered rounds will be K even for the bottom of the bag.

Rnd 1:   K
Rnd 2:   *K1, M1* (16 sts)
Rnd 4:   *K2, M1* (24 sts)
Rnd 6:   *K3, M1* (32 sts)
Rnd 8:   *K4, M1* (40 sts)
Rnd 10:   *K5, M1* (48 sts)
Rnd 12:   *K6, M1* (56 sts)
Rnd 13:   K

Bottom edge ridge:

Beginning with Rnd 14, switch to the 16" circular needle and PM at the beginning of the rnd. Add one strand each of Colors B, C, and D to the MC, and P around.

Rnds 15-17:   P

Folding over and creating the ridge:

Cut Colors B, C, and D, and continue with one strand of the MC. Fold over the edge ridge and secure it as follows:

Rnd 18:   Use a crochet hook to PU the first P bump on the WS in the last row where the MC only was used and place it on the LH needle. K it together with the first stitch on the LH needle. Continue to PU the first P bump below the next stitch on the LH needle, put it on the LH needle, and K it together with the next stitch to the end of the round.

Sides of the bag:

Rnd 19:   Knit in the round on 56 sts using one strand of the MC. Continue knitting until the work measures 12" from the folded back edge ridge (approximately 45 more rnds).

Picot Edge:

When the sides of the bag measure 12" from the folded back edge ridge, add one strand of Color E and knit 3 rnds. On rnd 4, create the fold line (eyelets) for the picot edge as follows:

K2tog, YO2 to the end of the rnd. Don't forget the YO2 after the last K2tog.
On the next rnd, *K1, then K into the first YO, letting the second loop of the YO2 drop* to the end of the rnd. K one additional rnd even, and then cut Color E and BO loosely with the MC only.

Leave a long enough yarn tail after binding off so that the picot edge can be hemmed. Fold the edging

to the inside of the bag on the fold line (eyelet row) and hem. Cut yarn and weave in ends.

I-cord wristlet strap:

With Color E and a US size 8 double pointed needle, CO 4 sts and work 16" of I-cord. BO.

Felting and finishing:

Place the bag into a pillow case and knot or pin the end shut. Using the lowest fill level on your washing machine, and the hottest water setting, place the pillow case into the machine along with a couple of heavy items like a pair of jeans and an old bath towel. These items will provide the necessary agitation for the item to felt well. Run the washing machine through a full normal cycle with water only (no detergent). If you have hard water which is not treated, you may want to add a small bit of fabric softener to the water at the beginning of the cycle.

When the cycle is complete, remove the bag from the pillow case and shape on a cylindrical object to dry, stretching as necessary to even up the top edge. For this bag, a 1.5 liter wine bottle is the perfect size for blocking.

When the bag is dry, install the six grommets according to manufacturer's instructions equidistant around bag so that the center of each grommet is 2" below the top of the bag.

Determine where the center back of the bag will be (between two of the grommets) and sew the ends of the I-cord wristlet strap at that point, centered between the grommets.

Draw the ribbon through the grommet eyes so that the two ends thread through to the outside of the bag opposite the center back. Draw up the top with the ribbon and tie into a bow.

Embellish the bag with stars embroidered with Color E and a tapestry needle.

February

Peekaboo Hearts

Materials:

2 balls (100 gr.) Crystal Palace Yarns Fjord in New Snow (MC)
3 balls (150 gr.) Crystal Palace Yarns Fjord in Fuchsia (Color B)
2 balls (100 gr.) Crystal Palace Yarns Fjord in Strawberry Pink (Color C)
1 26" US Size 11 (8.0 mm) circular needle
Stitch marker
Tapestry needle
1 magnetic purse closure
1 purchased purse handle
160 glue-on or sew-on sparkly acrylic heart-shaped "gems"
Fabric glue or sewing thread to apply "gems"

Dimensions:

Before felting – 11" tall, 11" wide, and 1½" deep
After felting – 6½" tall, 9" wide, and 1½" deep

Bottom of bag:

With the circular needle and one strand of the MC, CO 36 sts and work 12 rows of garter stitch (knit every row).

PU stitches for sides of bag:

After completing 12 rows of garter stitch (you should now have 6 garter ridges on the RS of your work), PU sts around the other three sides of the rectangle. PU 6 sts on the first short edge, 36 sts along the CO edge, and 6 more sts on the other short edge, to the first 36 sts on the needle (84 sts total). Place a marker to indicate this is the beginning point for all rnds.

Join and knit in the round on all 84 sts. When the work is 1½" from the rnd of PU sts (after approximately 5 rnds of knitting) P one rnd. This and future P rnds will be a built-in map for picking up ruffle stitches later on.

Continue knitting in the round using the following pattern of K and P rnds.

K 8 rnds, and then P 1 rnd until there are a total of 5 P rnds completed. After the 5th P rnd is worked, continue knitting in stockinette stitch (knit all rounds) until the work measures 11" from the PU sts. BO all sts and cut yarn.

Knitting the applied ruffles:

Work the ruffles one at a time from the top of the bag to the bottom of the bag alternating Color B, Color C, Color B, Color C, and finally end with Color B. To correctly orient the picked up sts, hold the bag on your lap with the open top nearest you and the bottom of the bag away from you. Insert the needle away from you through the P bump (staying on the RS of the work) and pull through a loop onto the LH needle.

With RS facing and one strand of Color B, begin at one corner to PU sts through each lower curve of the P bumps, for a total of 84 sts PU. PM to indicate the beginning of the rnd and work the ruffle as follows:

Rnd 1: K
Rnd 2: K
Rnd 3: *Kf/b* (168 sts)
Rnd 4: K
Rnd 5: K
Rnd 6: *Kf/b* (336 sts)
Rnd 7: K
Rnd 8: BO cut yarn.

Continue working the ruffles down the bag from top to bottom, alternating Color B and Color C and create a ruffle on each of the P rnds. 5 ruffles created.

Fabric for heart cut-outs:

The top of the bag is embellished with hearts cut from a knitted and felted swatch. Reserve enough of the MC for sewing on the purse handles, and then use what remains to knit fabric for the hearts. CO 30 sts and K in garter stitch until the MC is exhausted. Attach Color C and continue knitting until it is gone. Attach Color B and K until you have as much of Color B as Color C. BO.

Finishing:

Felt the bag and the swatch, and then shape them to dry. When thoroughly dry, apply the "gems" with a generous amount of fabric glue, or sew them on with sewing thread. Distribute the "gems" on the top and bottom of the ruffles, as well as on the body of the bag between the ruffles. Let the fabric glue dry completely.

Install the magnetic closure.

Cut out 2" tall heart shapes from the felted swatch (the bag in the photo used a total of 17 hearts). Use fabric glue to affix them to the front and back tops of the bag.

When the fabric glue has dried completely, use the reserved MC yarn to sew on the purse handles.

March to Your Own Music

Materials:

3 balls (150 gr.) Crystal Palace Yarns Taos in Gila Bend (MC)
1 ball (50 gr.) Crystal Palace Yarns Fjord in Aloe (Color B)
1 ball (50 gr.) Crystal Palace Yarns Fjord in Vine Green (Color C)
1 24" U.S. size #11 (8.0 mm) circular needle
2 U.S. size #11 (8.0 mm) double pointed needles
4 stitch markers, with one being a unique color
Tapestry needle
3 swivel hook purse rings for attaching strap ends
Purchased purse straps, backpack length (drapery tie-backs were used here)
1 magnetic clasp or other purse closure, if desired
Button or other embellishment for purse flap

Dimensions:

Before felting – 15" tall, 13 inches wide the bottom, 9½" wide the top, 4½"deep at the bottom, not including I-cord trim
After felting – 8" tall, 11" wide at the bottom, and 2¾" deep at the bottom, not including the I-cord trim

Gauge:

3½ sts per inch, 4 rows per inch worked with size #11 needle in stockinette stitch in the round

Bottom of Bag:

With one strand of MC and the circular needle, CO 44 sts and work flat in garter stitch for 32 rows. To make it easier to PU sts around the sides, K the rows so that each row starts with bringing the yarn to the front, slipping the first stitch P-wise, and then moving the yarn to the back. This will create an elongated stitch where sts will be PU for the sides of the bag.

K in garter stitch for 32 rows. Ending on the RS, PM and then PU 16 sts across the end of the rectangle using the slipped sts as your guideline. PM and PU 44 sts along the CO edge of the rectangle. PM and then PU 16 more sts from the remaining end. Place the uniquely colored marker after those 16 sts to denote the start of the round.

Body of the bag:

Knit in the round, as follows:

P1, K42, P1, K16 twice. The markers will serve as a reminder for you to P the first and last sts on the front and back of the bag. These columns of P sts will become a visual guide for where the applied I-cord will be knitted during finishing.

11

K until the bag measures 4" from the picked up sts, or approximately 16 rnds, before beginning to shape the bag with decs every 4th rnd. Each dec round will be worked as follows:

P1, SSK, K to the last 3 sts before the marker, K2tog, P1, K16 twice

Begin the dec section by working a dec rnd followed by 3 rnds of knitting every stitch. Continue knitting 1 dec rnd plus 3 plain rnds until there are 88 sts left on the needle (28 + 16 + 28 + 16).

When there are 88 sts left on the needle, continue knitting without additional dec until the bag measures 15" (approximately 60 rnds) from the picked up sts at the bottom.

Binding Off and Knitting the Flap:

On the last rnd of the bag, K28 and then BO the rest of the sts in the rnd, leaving the first 28 sts for the flap. Change to Color B and K back and forth in stockinette stitch on those 28 sts for 20 rows. Then:

Row 21:	K1, Kf/b, K to the last 2 sts on the needle, Kf/b, K1 (30 sts)
Row 22:	P
Row 23:	K
Row 24:	P
Row 25:	K1, Kf/b, K to the last 2 sts on the needle, Kf/b, K1 (32 sts)
Row 26:	P
Row 27:	K
Row 28:	P
Row 29:	K1, SSK, K to the last three sts on the needle, K2tog, K1
Row 30:	P1, P2tog, P to the last three sts on the needle, SSP, P1

Repeat Rows 29 and 30 until there are 6 sts on the needle, then: P1, P2tog, SSP, P1 (4 sts remain)

Next row: P2tog, SSP

This leaves 2 sts on the needle. Pass one over the other and BO the final stitch. Cut the yarn and weave in the tail.

Work the Fringe:

With Color C and RS facing, at the bottom edge of the flap PU 10 sts to the middle point of the flap, PU 3 sts in the corner (F/B/F of the same stitch), and then PU 10 more sts across the remaining bottom edge of the flap. K 3 more rows, ending with a WS row.

Turn, K1, then *CO 10 and BO 11* across all the sts to make the fringe. There should be one strand of fringe for each stitch in the last row knit. Cut yarn.

I-cord trim:

Beginning at the middle (point) of the flap and where the fringe row joins the flap, cast 3 sts onto one of the double pointed needles and work an applied I-cord across the flap bottom, up the side of the flap, down the back of the bag and across the bottom back, up the other side of the back, continuing down the other side of the flap and across the flap bottom to the point of beginning. Seam the two ends of the I-cord and fasten them to the bag so that a defined point is created.

Work a 3-stitch applied I-cord on the sides and bottom of the front of the bag as well.

Finishing:

Felt the bag using your preferred method. These yarns have a tendency to felt more than some. After the bag is felted, do not be afraid to pull and tug it into shape as you pin it out to dry. Keep working it until the correct shape is achieved.

When dry, affix the purse closure hardware and the backpack hardware and straps. Embellish the bag as you choose; the bag shown here was embellished with a kokopelli figure I created from polymer clay.

To create your own kokopelli figure (or any other shape), all you need to do is find a figure you like, make a copy of the design in the right size for the flap, and cut it out. Condition and roll out polymer clay and trace the figure onto the clay, then cut it out using a craft knife. Bake and finish according to manufacturer's instructions, and then affix it to your flap. Fabric glue was used here.

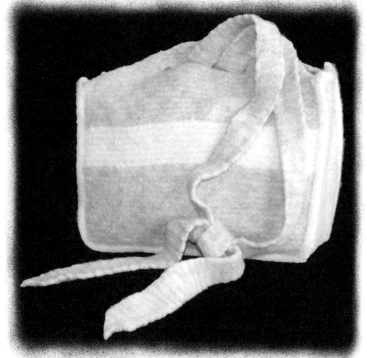

Baby Showers

Materials:

4 balls (400 gr.) Crystal Palace Yarns Iceland in Ice Storm (MC)
3 balls (300 gr.) Crystal Palace Yarns Iceland in Glacier Blue (Color B)
2 balls (200 gr.) Crystal Palace Yarns Iceland in New Snow (Color C)
1 US Size 15 (10.0 mm) knitting needle (straight or circular)
2 US Size 15 (10.0 mm) double pointed needles
Tapestry needle

Dimensions:

Before felting – 17" tall at the center point, 18 inches wide, 6"deep
After felting – 12" tall at the center point, 15" wide, and 5" deep

Gauge:

2½" sts per inch and 4½" rows in garter stitch

Back of Bag:

CO 45 sts using MC and work 32 rows in garter stitch. Change to Color C and work 14 more rows (46 total). Change back to MC and work 16 more rows (62 total) before shaping the top.

Shape the top over 18 rows as follows (all even rows are K):

Row 63   K1, SSK, K to the last 3 sts, K2tog, K1 (43 sts)
Row 65   K1, SSK, SSK, K to the last 5 sts, K2tog, K2tog, K1 (39)

Rows 67, 69, 71, 73, 75, 77, and 79, repeat Row 65. After Row 79, there will be 11 sts on the needle
Row 80   K
BO.

Front of Bag and Inside Divider Panel:

For the front of the bag, using MC, follow the instructions for the bag back, except as make a buttonhole as follows:

Row 69   K1, SSK, SSK, K5, BO15, K5, K2tog, K2tog, K1 (16 sts on needle)
Row 70   K8, CO15, K8 (31 sts)

Continue shaping and bind off as for the bag back.

For the inside divider panel, use Color B, CO 45 sts and work 62 rows in garter stitch. Shape in the same way as you did for the front of the bag. The front of the bag and the inside divider each have a buttonhole. The back of the bag does not.

Bottom of Bag:

CO 45 sts using Color B and work 28 rows in garter stitch. BO.

Side Gussets:

CO 15 sts using Color B and work 62 rows in garter stitch. BO. Make the second side gusset in the same way.

Strap:

Using MC, CO 7 sts and work in garter stitch for 276 rows. BO. Being careful not to twist the strap, sew both ends side by side securely to the inside back of the bag. Anchor the ends so that they are secured at the point where the shaping begins. Stitch again about 6 rows above that so they are doubly secured. The strap will pass through both buttonholes to become the shoulder strap. It will stretch during felting, and after the bag is shaped and dried, the strap can be cut in the middle and tied at the shoulder for your own preferred length.

Finishing:

Sew one side edge of the inside divider to the middle of the wrong side of one of the side gussets, being sure to keep the seam straight down the middle of the piece. Repeat for the other side gusset.

Sew the bottom edge of the inside divider to the middle row of the wrong side of the bag bottom.

Sew the bottom side edges to the bottom edges of the side gussets.

Sew the bag back to the bottom and side gussets. Repeat for the front.

Using the double pointed needles and Color C, work an applied I-cord around the sides and bottom of both the front and back, as well as across the top of the gusset between he front and the back.

Felt the bag using your preferred method and shape to dry. The straps here were cut into a point and then tied at the shoulder with a square knot. The divided sides can be used for a Mommy section and a Baby section. When worn cross-body with the bag on the back of the hip, both hands are free to hold baby.

May

May Bouquet

Materials:

3 balls (150 gr.) Crystal Palace Yarns Fjord in Vine Green (MC)
2 balls (100 gr.) Crystal Palace Yarns Merino Stripes in Sierra Moss (Color B)
1 ball (50 gr.) Crystal Palace Yarns Aran in Lichen (Color C)
1 ball (50 gr.) Crystal Palace Yarns Aran in Yellow Gold (Color D)
1 ball (50 gr.) Crystal Palace Yarns Aran in Ivory (Color E)
1 ball (50 gr.) Crystal Palace Yarns Aran in Dark Periwinkle (Color F)
1 ball (50 gr.) Crystal Palace Yarns Aran in Raspberry (Color G)
1 ball (50 gr.) Crystal Palace Yarns Aran in Light Blue (Color H)
1 ball (50 gr.) Crystal Palace Yarns Aran in Pale Pink (Color I)
1 24" US size #13 (9.0 mm) circular needle
1 US size #5 (3.75 mm) straight or short circular needle
1 set US size #5 (3.75 mm) double pointed needles
4 stitch markers, with one being a unique color
Tapestry needle

Sewing needle
Coordinating thread for sewing on embellishments or fabric glue

Dimensions:

Before felting – 10" wide at the base, 5" deep at the base, 15½" tall
After felting – 9" wide at the base, 4" deep at the base, 10" tall

Gauge:

2½ sts per inch in stockinette stitch in the round using 1 strand of Fjord and 1 strand of Merino Stripes and size #13 needle. 3 rows per inch.

Bottom of the bag:

With one strand of MC and one strand of Color B held together, use the larger circular needle to CO 24 sts and work 24 rows of garter stitch.

Body of the bag:

After the 24th row, PM and PU 12 sts across one end of the piece. PM and PU 24 sts along the CO edge. PM and PU 12 sts along the remaining side of the piece. Place the uniquely colored marker to denote the beginning of the rnd.

Work in the round in stockinette stitch. Work the specified increases and decreases on rnds 8, 16, 24, 32, 40, and 44. Work the buttonhole on rnds 42 and 43.

For rnds **8, 16, 24, and 32** –

K1, M1, K to the last stitch before the marker, M1, K1, Sl marker, K1, SSK, K to the last 3 sts before the marker, K2tog, K1, Sl marker twice.

For **Round 40 and subsequent rounds** –

Rnd 40   *K1, M1, K1, M1, K to the last 2 sts before the marker, M1, K1, M1, K1, Sl marker, SSK, K2tog, Sl marker* twice.

Rnd 42   *K12, BO 12, K14* twice

Rnd 43   *K12, CO 12, K14* twice

Rnd 44   *K1, M1, K1, M1, K to the last 2 sts before the marker, M1, K1, M1, K1, Sl marker, K2tog, Sl marker* twice.

After working rnd 44, work two more rnds even and then BO.

Calla Lily:

Using the size #5 needles, CO 15 with Color C. Work 8 rows in stockinette stitch and then cut Color C and attach Color E. K 4 rows in stockinette stitch and then shape as follows:

Row 13   K2, M1, K1, M1, K to 3 sts before the end, M1, K1, M1, K2
Row 14   P
Row 15   K
Row 16   P

Repeat Rows 13-16 once more (23 sts)

Row 21   K1, SSK, K to 3 sts before the end, K2tog, K1
Row 22   P

Repeat Rows 21 and 22 once more (19 sts)

Row 25   K1, Sl, K2tog, PSSO, K to 4 sts before the end, K2tog and ret to the LH needle, Sl the 2nd stitch on the LH needle over the first, Sl, K1 (15 sts)
Row 26   P

Repeat Rows 25 and 26 twice more (7 sts)

Row 31   SSK, K3, K2tog
Row 32   P
Row 33   SSK, K1, K2tog
Row 34   P
Row 35   K3tog, CO5, BO 6, cut yarn and pull through remaining loop.

To create the stamen for the flower, use Color D to CO 12 then BO 12, cut yarn and draw through the loop. Attach to the inside of the flower. Roll the bottom of the flower so that the ends meet and stitch together the green portion, leaving the white portion open.

Purple Coneflower:

With size #5 needle and Color F, CO 8 sts, PM, and join. Work in the round using your preferred method for small circumference knitting.

Rnd 1   K8
Rnd 2   *Kf/b* (16 sts)
Rnd 3   K
Rnd 4   K1 *CO10, BO 10, K1* until you have knitted the last stitch before the marker, then CO10 BO10.

(Tip: After the K1, use the backward E method to cast on the 10 stitches. Turn. Bind off 10 stitches, bring the yarn to front, slip the last stitch back to the LH needle that has the completed petals on it. Turn. Make sure petal is to the front, then K1. Before the K1, the number of petals completed plus the number of stitches remaining should equal 16. After this rnd, there should be 16 sts still on the needle, each at the base of a fringed cord.)

Rnd 5   K
Rnd 6   *K2tog* (8 sts)
Rnd 7   K8, cut yarn and pull through all 8 sts,
         draw up, and secure. Use the cast on tail
         to tighten the center of the flower.

With Color D and the size #5 needle, make a
bobble as follows and sew it to the center of the
flower.

Row 1   CO 1 and then work into the front and
         the back of that one stitch to make 7 sts.
Row 2   P
Row 3   K
Row 4   P
Row 5   K
Row 6   P
Row 7   SSK, K3, K2tog
Row 8   P
Row 9   SSK, K1, K2tog
Row 10   P3tog, cut yarn and pull through
         remaining loop.

Rosebuds:

Small – Use size #5 needle and Color I, CO 40 sts.
K 8 rows in stockinette stitch. Cut Color I and
attach Color C. Work 2 more rows. To BO and
create the rosebud, pass all the sts over the first
stitch on the needle, cut yarn and pull through the
remaining loop, drawing it up tightly. Twist the
piece into a spiral and stitch the sides to secure
them.

Medium – CO 50 sts with Color G. K 10 rows in
stockinette stitch. Cut Color G and attach Color C.
Work 2 more rows. BO and finish as for the small
rosebud.

Large – CO 60 sts with Color D. K 12 rows in
stockinette stitch. Cut Color D and attach Color C.
Work 4 more rows. BO and finish as for the small
rosebud.

Bluebells:

Make 4. With Color F and the size #5 needle, CO
20 sts. Work two rows in garter stitch, then cut
Color F and attach Color H.

Row 3 K2, Sl *K4, Sl* K2
Row 4 P2, Sl *P4, Sl* P2
Repeat Rows 3 and 4 twice more. Cut Color H and
attach Color C.

Row 9   Repeat Row 3
Row 10   P
Cut yarn and draw through all 20 sts on the needle.
Draw up tightly and seam together the two ends to
make a bluebell shape.

Camellia:

With Color E and the size #5 needle, CO 100 sts.

Row 1   K
Row 2   *K2tog*
Row 3   P
Row 4   *K2tog*
Row 5   P
Row 6   K
Cut yarn and pull through all 25 sts on the needle.
Seam the sides together. To make the center knot,
use Color D to CO15 then BO15. Tie into an
overhand knot, tuck the ends under the knot, and
sew it to the center of the camellia.

Stems:

With the size #5 double pointed needles, CO 3 sts
with Color C and work I-cord for approximately
50". BO.

Finishing:

Felt all pieces using your preferred method. Shape
the bag and flowers to dry. Cut 5 equal length
pieces (about 4" each) for the stems, and use the
remaining I-cord for any areas where stems would
be visible. Arrange the flowers and secure all
pieces to the bag with a sewing needle and
coordinating thread or fabric glue.

Alternate Color Yarns and Modifications

3 balls (150 gr.) Crystal Palace Yarns Fjord in Jet Black (MC)
2 balls (100 gr.) Crystal Palace Yarns Merino Frappe in Black (Color B)
1 ball (50 gr.) Crystal Palace Yarns Fjord in Vine Green (Color C)
1 ball (50 gr.) Crystal Palace Yarns Aran in Yellow Gold (Color D)
1 ball (50 gr.) Crystal Palace Yarns Fjord in Ivory (Color E)
1 ball (50 gr.) Crystal Palace Yarns Fjord in Fuchsia (Color F)
1 ball (50 gr.) Crystal Palace Yarns Fjord in Strawberry Pink (Color G)

Knit the bag the same as for the original design, substituting Alternate Colors MC and B.

Knit the Stems the same, substituting Alternate Color C.

Knit 5 Calla Lilies, substituting Alternate Colors C and E. Knit the stamens with Alternate Color D.

Knit 1 Bluebell with Alternate Color D for the cast on and first two rows. Switch to Alternate Color E through Row 8. Switch to Alternate Color C to finish.

Knit 1 small rosebud and 1 large rosebud with Alternate Colors F and C.

Knit 1 medium rosebud with Alternate Color F for 2 rows. Switch to Alternate Color G for 8 rows and the Alternate Color C to finish.

Curli-que (make 2) – Cast on 50 stitches to the size #5 needles in Alternate Color D. For the first row, *K2tog* to the end of the row. Turn and bind off. After felting, twist into a spiral curl and pin to dry.

Embellish the bag with the alternate flowers as illustrated in the photo.

June

Going to the Chapel

Materials:

2 balls (200 gr.) Crystal Palace Yarns Iceland in
Ivory
1 ball (50 gr.) Crystal Palace Yarns Fjord in Ice
Storm
1 ball (25 gr.) Crystal Palace Yarns Kid Merino in
Misty Blue (divide into two balls)
Needles: 1 40" US size 13 (9 mm) for Magic Loop
Method **-OR-** 2 24" US size 13 (9 mm) for 2 circular
needle method **-OR-** 1 set of US size 13 (9 mm)
double pointed needles **-AND-**
2 US size 7 (4.5 mm) double pointed needles for
knitting I-cord
2 different colored stitch markers
1 tapestry needle
Pearl beads
Coordinating sewing thread and needle for applying
pearls
1 magnetic snap or other hidden purse closure
2 purse loops for fastening the strap

Gauge:

3 sts per inch and 4 rows per inch in stockinette
stitch worked in the rnd with Iceland and size #13
needles.

Dimensions:

Before felting –   12" wide at bottom, 10" wide at
    the top, and 11" tall. Flap is 8½" x 3¾"
    before felting (exclusive of ruffle). Ruffle
    is 3" deep before felting.
After felting –   8½" tall, 11" wide at the bottom,
    9" wide at the top. Flap is 3" wide
    (exclusive of ruffle). Ruffle is 2" deep.

Body of Bag:

Several methods could be used to knit this bag in
the round. The method used here was Magic
Loop; however, the two circular needle method or
double pointed needles will work as well. CO 68 sts
using your preferred method of knitting in the
round. A closed bottom CO is described below for
those who choose to use either 2 circular needles or
the Magic Loop method.

Closed Bottom Cast On with two circular needles or Magic Loop method –

The Magic Loop method is the technique of using one long circular needle to knit items with a small circumference. It or the two circular needle method is recommended here as the easiest way to knit this bag, and is adaptable to any small-circumference knitting. The Closed Bottom CO used here will result in a seamless bottom for the bag which would require no additional sewing upon completion.

A nice online tutorial of the Magic Loop method of knitting, with photos, is found at this link: http://www.az.com/~andrade/K/mloop.html

To summarize how to CO, we will:

• Hold both ends of the circular needle in the right hand (Magic Loop) or hold two circular needles parallel to one another in the right hand.
• Alternately CO sts with the backward loop method onto each needle.
• Begin knitting.

Easy! So here's how to do it.

With the long circular needle (or two shorter circular needles) and one strand of Iceland, make a slip knot in the yarn and place it on one of the needle ends. Bring the needle ends together in your right hand so that they are parallel, with one holding the slip knot. Arrange them so that the top needle holds the knot and the other needle is next to it. We will call these Needle 1 (with the knot) and Needle 2.

With the working yarn, and using the backward loop method, CO one stitch to Needle 2 (now there is one stitch on each needle). Proceed to CO sts, one to Needle 1 and then one to Needle 2 using the backward loop method until each needle holds 34 sts (total 68). The CO sts should be snug, but not overly tight, as they will tighten slightly with the first rnd of knitting. The yarn criss-crosses between the needles, holding them close together and creating a closed seamless bottom.

For Magic Loop, orient the needle as follows – Needle tips pointing to the right, the loop of the needle's cable to the left, and with the working yarns coming up between the two needle tips from

the last CO stitch on the back needle (Needle 2). Needle 1 should have the beginning yarn tail dangling at the far left and is closest to your body. Half the sts are on Needle 1 and half are on Needle 2 You are ready to begin knitting.

Pull the tip of Needle 2 (back needle) and let the sts slide onto the cable. Pull it out far enough so that you can then comfortably hold it in your right hand and begin knitting the sts from Needle 1 while still keeping the two sets of sts separated by the looped cable. K 34 sts. The first half of Rnd 1 is now finished.

To K the second half of Rnd 1, turn the needle so the tips are once again pointing right, push the front needle into the sts you have not yet knitted so they are at the tip and ready to K, and pull the back needle out of the sts you have just finished knitting (sliding them back onto the cable) so you have a working needle to use. K 34. Rnd 1 completed. Turn the needle so the tips are again pointing right and you will be ready to begin Rnd 2. Always be sure that when you begin to K each half of the rnd, the working yarn is coming up between the points of the needle tips so that it doesn't create a YO (and then later become an extra stitch on the needle). As you K, after about 4 rnds, you will see that the P side of the knitting (WS) can be pushed down so the stockinette side (RS) is more clearly visible as the outside of the work and the bag begins to take its shape. Just pay close attention to what you are doing, take it one step at a time, and you soon will have mastered a valuable knitting technique.

For those who prefer to knit with double pointed needles or one small circumference circular needle, simply CO 68 sts, mark the beginning of your rnd, and proceed with an open bottom that will be seamed during finishing.

Continue to knit the bag as follows:

Knit a total of 40 rnds in stockinette stitch, making decreases on rnds 13, 22, and 31. Work dec rnds as follows:

K1, SSK, K to the last three sts on the first half of the rnd, then K2tog, repeating for the second half of the rnd. After rnd 31, there will be 56 sts left on the needle.

After working rnd 40, BO all but the last stitch. You will be at one of the side edges. Leaving the last stitch on the needle, transfer it to a size #13 double pointed needle and CO two more sts using the backward loop method. Work an applied I-cord down the side, across the bottom edge, and up the other side of the bag. Cut yarn, pull end through all three sts on the needle, and secure the yarn tail.

Make purse flap:

With one strand of the Iceland and the size #13 needle, CO 6 sts and work the flap as follows:

Row 2:	P
Row 3:	K1, M1, K to the last stitch, M1, K1 (8 sts)
Row 4:	P
Row 5:	K1, M1, K1, M1, K to the last two sts, M1, K1, M1, K1 (12 sts)
Row 6:	P
Rows 7-28:	Work in stockinette stitch
Row 29:	K1, Sl, K2togTBL, PSSO, K to the last 4 sts, K2tog and place back on the LH needle, pass the 2nd stitch on the LH needle over the one slipped back, Sl, K1 (8 sts)
Row 30:	P
Row 31:	K1, SSK, K2, K2tog, K1 (6 sts)
Row 32:	P
BO.	

Ruffle – Using 1 strand of Fjord and two strands of Kid Merino held together, PU 44 sts around the flap. Place marker and K one rnd.

Rnd 2:	*K1, M1* (88 sts)
Rnds 3-5:	K
Rnd 6	*K1, M1* (176 sts)
Rnds 7-8:	K
Rnd 9:	*K2, M1* (352 sts)
Rnd 10:	K
BO.	

Make shoulder strap:

Using the size #7 double pointed needles, CO 3 sts using the Fjord and two strands of the Kid Merino held together. Work an I-cord that is 40" before felting.

Finishing:

Felt the bag, flap, and shoulder strap, and shape to dry. Sew on the flap across the purse opening, leaving it longer in front than in the back. Embellish the base of the ruffle with a row of sewn on pearls as shown. Apply the magnetic closure. Double the shoulder strap and make a love knot at the top center of the cords. Sew on the purse loops and secure the ends of the strap to the loops.

Materials:

2 balls (100 gr.) Crystal Palace Yarns Fjord in Rose Petal (MC)
1 ball (50 gr.) Crystal Palace Yarns Fjord in Ivory (Color B)
2 balls (100 grams Crystal Palace Yarns Fjord in Fern (Color C)
3 26" US size 11 (8.0 mm) circular knitting

needles, or 2 circular and 1 pair of straight needles
Purchased purse handle
Teardrop shaped glass beads
Sewing thread
Sewing needle or beading needle (or fabric glue if preferred)
Purse closure hardware

Dimensions:

Before felting – 18½" wide x 12" tall (at the center, 14" at the highest point)
After felting – 16½" wide x 8½" tall (at the center)

Bag Side 1:

An interesting feature of this bag is that after the half circle is made with the MC, you will pick up stitches and knit extra rows across the top to add length to the piece before adding the white and green sections. This method helps to compensate for the higher ratio of vertical shrinkage.

With one of the circular needles and one strand of MC, CO 4 sts. Increase on even rows. Knit flat in

garter stitch. Unless noted otherwise, all odd numbered rows are K even.

Row 1:   K
Row 2:   K1, M1, Kf/b, Kf/b, M1, K1 (8 sts)
Row 4:   K2, M1, K1, M1, K2, M1, K1, M1, K2 (12 sts)
Row 6:   K3, M1, K2, M1, K2, M1, K2, M1, K3 (16 sts)
Row 8:   K4, M1, K2, M1, K4, M1, K2, M1, K4 (20 sts)
Row 10: K5, M1, K3, M1, K4, M1, K3, M1, K5 (24 sts)
Row 12: K6, M1, K3, M1, K6, M1, K3, M1, K6 (28 sts)
Row 14: K7, M1, K4, M1, K6, M1, K4, M1, K7 (32 sts)

Row 16: K8, M1, K4, M1, K8, M1, K4, M1, K8 (36 sts)

Row 18: K9, M1, K5, M1, K8, M1, K5, M1, K9 (40 sts)

Row 20: K10, M1, K5, M1, K10, M1, K5, M1, K10 (44 sts)

Row 22: K11, M1, K6, M1, K10, M1, K6, M1, K11 (48 sts)

Row 24: K12, M1, K6, M1, K12, M1, K6, M1, K12 (52 sts)

Row 26: K13, M1, K7, M1, K12, M1, K7, M1, K13 (56 sts)

Row 28: K14, M1, K7, M1, K14, M1, K7, M1, K14 (60 sts)

Row 30: K15, M1, K8, M1, K14, M1, K8, M1, K15 (64 sts)

Row 32: K16, M1, K8, M1, K16, M1, K8, M1, K16 (68 sts)

Row 34: K17, M1, K9, M1, K16, M1, K9, M1, K17 (72 sts)

Row 36: K18, M1, K9, M1, K18, M1, K9, M1, K18 (76 sts)

Row 38: K19, M1, K10, M1, K18, M1, K10, M1, K19 (80 sts)

Row 40: K20, M1, K10, M1, K20, M1, K10, M1, K20 (84 sts ending on a RS row)

At this point, because felting shrinks more vertically than it does horizontally, you will add more height to the piece. RS facing, yarn still attached, leave the 84 sts on the cable. With another circular needle, PU 42 sts across the straight top of the work. K in garter stitch for 10 rows after picking up the sts, ending on a RS row. BO 41 sts. The 42nd stitch will become the pivot stitch for picking up the next sts.

Transfer that last stitch to the RH needle of the held sts. PU 5 additional sts across the narrow end of the extra length you have just completed. 6 sts are on the RH needle and all the held sts are on the LH needle. K 84, then PU 6 sts across the other narrow end of the knitted extension.

Switch to Color B and work six garter stitch rows as follows:

Row 1: K27, M1, *K21, M1* twice, then K27 for a total of 99 sts

Row 2: K

Row 3: K28, M1, K22, M1, K21, M1, K28 for a total of 102 sts

Row 4: K

Row 5: K29, M1, K22, M1, K22, M1, K29 for a total of 105 sts

Row 6: K

Change to Color C and work 14 rows in garter stitch as follows:

Row 1: K30, M1, K24, M1, K24, M1, K27 for a total of 108 sts

Row 2: K (Stop here if you are knitting Side 2 of the bag)

Rows 3-14: K

Hold these sts on the circular needle while you work Side 2 on another circular needle.

Bag Side 2:

Repeat as for side 1, stopping where noted.

Finishing:

With right sides together, join the two curved sides of the bag around the outside of the semi-circle using a 3-needle bind-off.

Felt the bag and shape it to dry.

With a matching color thread, or invisible nylon thread, sew on the teardrop beads to simulate the watermelon seeds on the front and back sides. Alternatively, fabric glue can be used.

Sunny Funflower

Materials:

1 ball (50 gr.) Crystal Palace Yarns Nubbles in
Jet Black (MC)
1 ball (50 gr.) Crystal Palace Yarns Fjord in
Tree Bark (Color B)
2 balls (100 gr.) Crystal Palace Yarns Aran in
Lichen (Color C)
1 ball (50 gr.) Crystal Palace Yarns Aran in
Yellow Gold (Color D)
1 ball (25 gr.) Crystal Palace Yarns Kid
Merino in Lemon Sherbet (Color E)
1 ball (50 gr.) Crystal Palace Yarns Deco
Ribbon in Celery (Color F)
1 16" US size #11 (8.0 mm) circular needle
1 set US size #11 (8.0 mm) double pointed
needles
1 US size #8 (5.0 mm) double pointed
needles
1 ladybug button
Sewing needle and thread (for button)
Stitch markers
Tapestry needle
Purchased closure hardware, if desired.

Dimensions:

Before felting – 13" in diameter (bag only)
After felting – 7" in diameter (bag only)

Front of bag/center of flower:

Using the double pointed needle, or your preferred
method for knitting small circumference items, CO 8 sts
with one strand of MC and one strand of Color B held
together. Distribute sts on needles, PM, join, and work
in the round as follows:

Rnd 1:   P
Rnd 2:   *P1, M1* (16 sts)
Rnd 3:   P
Rnd 4:   *P2, M1* (24 sts)
Rnd 5:   P
Rnd 6:   *P3, M1* (32 sts)
Rnd 7:   P
Rnd 8:   *P4, M1* (40 sts)
Rnd 9:   P
Rnd 10:   Cut MC and then proceed with Color B to
K5, M1 (48 sts)

Rnd 11:   P, cut Color B, and attach Color C (This sets up the round of P bumps through which the innermost layer of flower petals will be picked up.)

Rnd 12:   With Color C, *K6, M1* (56 sts)

Rnd 13:   P (This sets up the round of P bumps through which the outer layer of flower petals will be picked up.)

Rnd 14:   *K7, M1* (64 sts)

Rnd 15:   K

Rnd 16:   *K8, M1* (72 sts)

Rnd 17:   K

Rnd 18:   *K9, M1* (80 sts)

Rnd 19:   K

Rnd 20:   *K10, M1* (88 sts)

Rnd 21:   K

Rnd 22:   *K11, M1* (96 sts)

Rnd 23:   K

Rnd 24:   *K12, M1* (104 sts

Rnd 25:   K

Shape top and work sides:

BO 26 sts, K88. Working back and forth, knit in stockinette stitch for 4 rows. Begin by turning and working a P row. At the end of the 4th row (RS facing) CO 26 sts, PM, and join. Resume working in the round for the back of the bag.

Back of bag:

K 1 rnd and then begin decreasing the back of the bag on the even rounds. Follow each dec rnd with a rnd of plain knitting.

Rnd 2:   *K:11, K2tog* (96 sts) .

Rnd 4:   *K10, K2tog* (88 sts)

Rnd 6:   *K9, K2tog* (80 sts)

Rnd 8:   *K8, K2tog* (72 sts)

Rnd 10: *K7, K2tog* (64 sts)

Rnd 12: *K6, K2tog* (56 sts)

Rnd 14: *K5, K2tog* (48 sts)

Rnd 16: *K4, K2tog* (40 sts)

Rnd 18: *K3, K2tog* (32 sts)

Rnd 20: *K2, K2tog* (24 sts)

Rnd 22: *K1, K2tog* (16 sts)

Rnd 24: *K2tog* (8 sts)

Rnd 25: K8, cut yarn and draw it through all 8 sts on the needle. Weave in ends.

Flower Petals:

Knit flower petals with one strand of Color D and one strand of Color E held together throughout.

Pick up petal stitches on the two rounds that were purled for that purpose. Work the bottom layer on the outermost rnd, and the top layer on the innermost rnd.

Bottom layer – With the circular needle, RS facing work through the stitch toward the center of the front and PU 56 sts for the bottom layer first. After picking up the sts, join, and K one rnd. Transfer the first 7 sts to a size #11 double pointed needle and leave the other sts held on the circular needle. K each petal on the double pointed needles back and forth as follows:

Row 1:   K7

Row 2:   P7

Row 3:   K1, M1, K5, M1, K1 (9 sts)

Row 4:   P9

Row 5:   K1, M1, K to the last stitch, M1, K1 (11 sts)

Row 6:   P11

Row 7:   K11

Row 8:   P11

Row 9:   K11

Row 10: P11

Row 11: K1, SSK, K to the last three sts, K2tog, K1 (9 sts)

Row 12: P9

Row 13: K1, SSK, K to the last three sts, K2tog, K1 (7 sts)

Row 14: P7

Row 15: K1, SSK, K to the last three sts, K2tog, K1 (5 sts)

Row 16: P5

Row 17: K1, SSK, K2tog (3 sts)

Row 18: P3

Row 19: K3

Row 20: P3

Row 21: SSK, K1 (2 sts)

Row 22:   P2tog, cut yarn and pull through the remaining loop. With the yarn tail, tack the very tip of the petal to the bag so that the tips are lined up around the bag just below the bag opening and just to the front of the side edge (approximately 13 or 14 rows above the picked up sts)

Repeat for the remaining sts held on the circular needle (8 petals made)

Top layer – With the circular needle, RS facing, PU 48 sts for the top layer of petals on the innermost round of purl bumps. You may begin picking up the sts anywhere along the rnd, or you may prefer to begin so that the petals will be centered between the bottom petals. After picking up the sts, join, and K one rnd. Transfer the first 6 sts to a size #11 double pointed needle and leave the other sts held on the circular needle. K each petal on the double pointed needles back and forth as follows:

Row 1:   K6
Row 2:   P6
Row 3:   K1, M1, K to the last stitch, M1, K1 (8 sts)
Row 4:   P8
Row 5:   K1, M1, K to the last stitch, M1, K1 (10 sts)
Row 6:   P10
Row 7:   K10
Row 8:   P10
Row 9:   K10
Row 10:   P10
Row 11:   K1, SSK, K to the last three sts, K2tog, K1 (8 sts)
Row 12:   P8
Row 13   K1, SSK, K to the last three sts, K2tog, K1 (6 sts)
Row 14:   P6
Row 15:   K1, SSK, K2tog, K1 (4 sts)
Row 16:   P4
Row 17:   K4
Row 18:   P4
Row 19:   SSK, K2tog (2 sts)
Row 20:   P2tog, cut yarn and pull through the remaining loop. Weave in ends.

Repeat for the remaining sts held on the circular needle (8 petals made)

Handle Carrier Loops:

With size #11 needles and Color C, PU 8 sts a few rows below the side of the bag opening and work 12 rows in stockinette stitch. BO and sew the flap, WS together, to the base of the flap at the line of picked up sts. Repeat for the other side.

Leaves:

Make two leaves (or as many as you like). Using size #11 needles, CO 4 sts with Color C.

Rows 1-4:   Work in stockinette stitch on 4 sts
Row 5:   K1, M1, K to the last stitch, M1, K1 (6 sts)
Rows 6-8:   Work in stockinette stitch on 6 sts
Row 9:   K1, M1, K to the last stitch, M1, K1 (8 sts)
Rows 10-12:   Work in stockinette stitch on 8 sts
Row 13:   K1, M1, K to the last stitch, M1, K1 (10 sts)
Rows 14-20:   Work in stockinette stitch on 10 sts
Row 21:   K1, M1, K to the last stitch, M1, K1 (12 sts)
Rows 22-32:   Work in stockinette stitch on 12 sts
Row 33:   K1, SSK, K to the last 3 sts, K2tog, K1 (10 sts)
Rows 34-36:   Work in stockinette stitch on 10 sts
Row 37:   K1, SSK, K to the last 3 sts, K2tog, K1 (8 sts)
Row 38:   P
Row 39:   K1, SSK, SSK, K2tog, K2tog, K1 (4 sts)
Row 40:   P
Row 41:   SSK, K2tog, Pass the rightmost stitch on the RH needle over the leftmost stitch, cut yarn, and pull the end through the loop.

Purse Handle (non-felted):

With size #8 double pointed needles and Color F, CO 4 sts and knit 40" of I-cord. BO, leaving tails long enough on both ends to sew the handle to the leaves after they are felted.

Finishing:

Felt the bag and leaves and shape to dry. To keep the carrier loops open, insert a clean wine cork into each loop (secured with a straight pin through the cork, if necessary) so it will not felt closed.

The center of the flower will naturally bow out and have a 3-D effect to it. Support it with a crumpled plastic market bag during the drying process. When dry, sew on the ladybug button with the coordinating thread and sewing needle. If desired, tack the sunflower leaves around the top to the underneath layer so they do not flop over. Draw the purse handle through the carrier loops, crossing the ends through one side. Overlap each end onto the wide end of a leaf and sew using the tails of the purse handle and a tapestry needle. Sew on purchased closure hardware, if desired.

September

Back to Work/Back to School Brown Bag

Materials:

3 balls (300 gr.) Crystal Palace Yarns Iceland in Tree Bark (MC)
1 ball (100 gr.) Crystal Palace Yarns Iceland in Teal Lake (Color B)
1 ball (50 gr.) Crystal Palace Yarns Little Flowers in Sea Foam
1 ball (50 gr.) Crystal Palace Yarns Fjord in Tree Bark (Color D)
1 ball (50 gr.) Crystal Palace Yarns Fjord in Teal Lake (Color E)
1 26" US size #13 (9.0 mm) circular needle
4 stitch markers, one of which is a unique color
1 set US size #13 (9.0 mm) double pointed needles
2 US size #8 (5.0 mm) double pointed needles
½ yard of wide coordinating ribbon
½ yard of 1/4" coordinating ribbon
Tapestry needle
Sewing needle
Large button (This one was made from polymer clay to match the bag.)
Coordinating thread for sewing on ribbon, button, and dots (or fabric glue, if preferred)

Dimensions:

Before felting – 7½" deep, 12½" wide, and 14½" tall
After felting – 6 ½" deep, 10" wide, and 10" tall

Bottom of Bag:

With the circular needle and MC, CO 30 sts and work back and forth in garter stitch. To make it easier to PU sts around the sides, K the rows so that each row starts with the yarn to the front. Slip the first stitch P-wise and then move the yarn to the back. This creates an elongated stitch where the new sts can be picked for the sides of the bag. K in garter stitch for 30 rows.

End on the RS, PM and then PU 15 sts across the end of the rectangle using the slipped sts as your guideline. PM and PU 30 sts along the CO edge of the rectangle. PM and PU 15 more sts from the remaining end. Place the uniquely colored marker after those 15 sts to denote the start of the rnd.

Body of Bag:

Join and knit in the round, working every row as follows:

P1, K28, P1, K15 twice. The markers are a reminder to P the first and last sts on the front and back of the bag. These columns of P sts will be a guide for knitting the applied I-cord at the end. K until the bag measures 14" from the picked up sts. On the last rnd, work as follows:

P1, K28, P1, K15, P30, K15

Cut MC and continue knitting with Color B and one strand of Color C. K as before for 4 additional rnds. After the 4th rnd, bind off, leaving live sts for the handles, as follows:

BO7, K4, BO8, K4, BO22 twice. Leave the 4 sets of 4 live sts on the cable of the circular needles.

Handles:

With the double pointed needles and MC, work I-cord on 4 of the sts. Work until the cord is 16" long and then graft it to the other 4 live sts on the same side of the bag. Repeat for the other side.

Flap:

The row of purled sts is on the back side of the bag. Pick up flap stitches on this row of P sts. With Color B and one strand of Color C, the circular needle and RS facing, PU 30 sts on the P bumps across the bag. Insert the needle from bottom to top and pull a loop of yarn through and onto the RH needle. Work 7 rows on these 30 sts in stockinette stitch. Make the opening where the handles come through in the following manner:

Row 8   K7, BO16, K7
Row 9   P7, CO16, P7

Continue knitting in stockinette stitch for 5" more after Row 9. BO.

I-cord Edging:

Place the bag in your lap, RS facing and top nearest you, bottom facing away from you. Begin on the right hand side. K one continuous applied I-cord down the side, around to the back, up and around the flap edge, and then down the other side of the back, around the bottom to the front and back up to the top. To do this, CO 3 sts to one of the double pointed needles with one strand of Color B only and then insert the tip of the needle into the first P bump in the column of P sts at the front corner of the bag. Pull the bump onto the needle as the picked up stitch, followed by the 3 CO sts. Transfer the needle with the sts to your left hand and work the I-cord as follows: K2, K2togTBL. Knitting the last two sts together through the back loop will cause the CO stitch to twist over the top of the picked up stitch so it will not show.

On the left end of the needle, PU the next P bump down the column, slide the sts to the right end of the needle and continuing knitting the I-cord in the same manner, knitting the first two sts and then knitting the last two sts together through the back loop. Continue around the front, bottom, and back, and then proceed around the flap edge and the other side edges in one continuous applied I-cord. When you reach the other side of the top front of the bag, cut the yarn and pull it through the 3 sts on the needle and weave the end into the WS of the top.

Polka Dots:

With Color D and size #8 double pointed needles, CO 4 sts and work I-cord for at least 48". Repeat with Color E.

Finishing:

Felt the bag and I-cords and shape to dry. Use the ribbon to create a strap, a keep, a button loop, and a button placket. Sew on the placket with the button applied to the top of it. Sew the top ribbon strap to the back bottom edge of the purse flap so it comes across the buttonhole through the handles, through the keep and then fastens around the button. With the I-cords, make assorted sizes of spiral polka dots. Sew or glue the dots onto their opposite colors in a random manner.

You can easily make your own polymer clay button. This one was made using one layer of brown, one layer of blue, and one layer of sparkly silver clay, one on top of the other, then rolled jelly-roll fashion and sliced ¼" thick. Bake and finish according to manufacturer's instructions.

October Changing Leaves

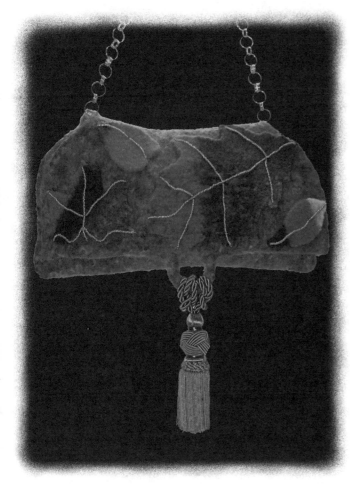

Materials:

3 balls (150 gr.) Crystal Palace Yarns Fjord in Flame (MC)
3 balls (150 gr.) Crystal Palace Yarns Fjord in Fall Herbs (Color B)
1 ball (50 gr.) Crystal Palace Yarns Fjord in Mandarin Orange (Color C)
1 ball (50 gr.) Crystal Palace Yarns Fjord in Vine Green (Color D)
1 ball (50 gr.) Crystal Palace Yarns Fjord in Tree Bark (Color E)
1 ball (50 gr.) Crystal Palace Yarns Fjord in Ivory (Color F)
1 US size 15 (10.0mm) circular needle at least 40" long or 2 24" circular needles
2 US size 15 (10.0 mm) double pointed needles
2 stitch markers of different colors
Closure hardware, if desired
Beaded wire for embellishing leaves
Beading needle and monofilament thread for sewing on beads
Sewing needle and coordinating thread or fabric glue
Purchased chain for shoulder strap
Purchased drapery tassel for bottom of flap

Dimensions:

Before felting – 16" wide at the bottom, 11½" tall, 11½" wide, flap is 8½" tall
After felting – 14" wide at the bottom, 8" tall, flap is 6½" tall

Gauge:

2½ sts per inch worked in stockinette stitch in the round with size #15 needle, 3½ rows per inch

Casting on:

Use one long circular or two shorter circulars and one strand each of MC and Color B. Use the Turkish Cast On method or the Figure 8 method to CO a total of 80 sts. Place a marker to denote the beginning of the rnd, K40, place a marker to mark the other edge of the bag, and K40 back to the beginning of the rnd. Work 26 rnds and then shape the top of the bag as follows (K all even rnds):

Rnd 27 *K1, SSK, K to the last three sts before the marker, K2tog, K1* twice (76)
Rnd 29 Repeat Rnd 27 (72)
Rnd 31 *K1, Sl, SSK, PSSO, K to the last 4 sts before the marker and then K2tog, return the stitch to the LH needle and then pass the 2nd stitch on the LH needle over the stitch just returned, Sl that stitch to the RH needle* twice (64)
Rnd 33 Repeat Rnd 31 (56)
Rnd 35 Repeat Rnd 27 (52)

Flap:

BO 26 sts along the front of the bag between the markers. Work the flap in stockinette stitch for 4 rows, then shape as follows (P all even rows):

Row 5   K1, M1, K to the last stitch before the
         end, M1, K1 (28)
Row 7   Repeat Row 5 (30)
Row 9   K1, M1, K1, M1, K to the last 2 sts
         before the end, M1, K1, M1, K1 (34)
Row 11   Repeat Row 9 (38)
Row 13   Repeat Row 5 (40)

After inc to 40 sts, work 17 more rows in stockinette stitch.

Bind Off:

RS facing, BO 17 sts. Work I-cord using the next 3 sts as the first row (transfer to a double pointed needle, K3, then begin working I-cord) for 12 rows. Graft the 3 sts of the I-cord to the next three sts of the flap using a 3-needle BO, then BO the remaining 17 sts of the flap.

Leaves:

Use the remaining yarns to knit small swatches, combining strands of the various yarns to produce different color combinations. For instance, MC + Color E; Color F + Color B. Use any color combinations that will result in gradations of colors. Sew the pieces together in a crazy quilt fashion so they turn different directions and when felted produce a piece of fabric from which your leaves will be cut. Make the fabric piece large enough to cut out the number of leaves you want to place on the flap. As illustrated here, swatches used a CO of 15 and then were worked between 10 and 20 rows to get various sizes and shapes of knitted patchwork. The more willy-nilly they are sewn together, the more fun looking leaves you'll get.

Felting and finishing:

Felt the bag and the fabric piece using your preferred method. Pin out, shape, and dry the bag and the piece on a blocking board.

Leaf shapes can be taken from actual leaves in your yard; just go out and find shapes you like. If necessary, reduce or enlarge them on a copying machine, and then use for a pattern. Or, find leaf shapes you like in books or on the internet. Place the leaf shape on the fabric piece and pin or trace the shape, and cut it out. Lay out the leaves so that a good variety of the color ways will be apparent in the leaf. Use pinking shears to make a nice serrated edge for some of the leaves. Sew or glue the leaves to the flap, and then use the beaded wire to create veins in the leaves. Tack down the beaded wire at intervals to secure it firmly. If desired, install closure hardware on the bag. Attach shoulder strap and drapery tassel as illustrated.

Knitting Together a Family

November

In honor of National Adoption Month

This bag is special to me because it's a representation of our family. Our three children were adopted, one in a domestic open adoption, and two through international adoption in Guatemala. The three strands of yarn that make the stripes in the bag are light, medium, and darker tan, just like our children. The bands of Splash yarn make a nice furry stripe at intervals, representing the warm and fuzzy love that binds us all together.

The gusset of this purse is pleated and shaped flat to dry. But like a family, this purse is expandable to accommodate more than you think it can hold. It was knitted together with love in honor of National Adoption Month, just as our family was knitted together with love through adoption.

Materials:

3 balls (150 gr.) Crystal Palace Yarns Fjord in Sand (MC)
2 balls (100 gr.) Crystal Palace Yarns Merino Frappe in Mink (Color B)
2 balls (100 gr.) Crystal Palace Yarns Merino Stripes in Sandstorm (Color C)
1 ball (100 gr.) Crystal Palace Yarns Splash in Mink (Color D)
1 US size #15 (10.0 mm) circular needle, 24" or longer
Tapestry needle to weave in ends
Stitch marker
Purchased purse handle and purse hooks
Magnetic snap or other closure hardware

Dimensions:

Before felting – 15½" tall, 13" wide, 5" deep
After felting – 11" tall, 12" wide, 4" deep

Gauge:

2.2 sts per inch in stockinette stitch worked flat with size #15 needles and one strand each of MC and Colors B and C
2.5 rows per inch

Bottom of Bag:

Use one strand each of MC, Color B, and Color C. CO 28 sts and work 15 rows of stockinette stitch.

Body of Bag:

RS facing, PU 14 sts along one side edge of the piece, 28 sts along the CO edge, and 14 sts along the other side edge of the piece. PM to denote the beginning of the rnd. Begin knitting the stripe pattern –

K 5 rnds with MC, Color B, and Color C held together. Drop MC, add one strand of Color D, and K 2 rnds.

Repeat the stripe sequence 5 more times and then work 5 rnds with MC, Color B, and Color C held together. BO.

Finishing:

Felt the bag using your preferred method. Shape the bag laid out on a blocking board, pleat in the sides and bottom, and pin into shape to dry. This creates a pleated gusset on the sides and bottom.

Attach the purse handle and closure hardware.

December

Santa's Got a Brand New Bag

Materials:

4 balls (400 gr.) Crystal Palace Yarns Iceland in Red Cerise (MC)
1 ball (100 gr.) Crystal Palace Yarns Iceland in Ivory (Color B)
1 ball (100 gr.) Crystal Palace Yarns Splash in Ivory (Color C)
1 ball (50 gr.) Crystal Palace Yarns Fizz Stardust in White Ice (Color D)
1 ball (50 gr.) Crystal Palace Yarns Deco-Ribbon in White (Color E)
US size #15 (10.0 mm) double pointed and/or circular needles, changing as necessary as the diameter of the bag increases
2 US size #7 (4.5 mm) double pointed needles
1 stitch marker
8 silver-toned ½" grommets and setting tool
2 purse hooks with openable clasps, silver-toned
2 twisted cord drapery tie-backs, one in red and one in white

Dimensions:

Before felting – 13"diameter at the bottom of the bag x 23" tall
After felting – 10" diameter at the bottom of the bag x 14" tall x 37" in circumference

Gauge:

2½" sts per inch in stockinette in the round with Size #15 needle and 3 rows per inch

Bottom of the Bag:

Use size #15 double pointed needles or your favorite small circumference knitting method. CO 8 sts with 1 strand of MC. PM, join sts being careful not to twist them, and K one rnd. Later, weave in the tail to tighten any potential hole in the bottom of the bag. Increase as follows:

Rnd 2: *K1, M1*
Rnd 3 and all odd rnds until the bottom is finished: Knit
Rnd 4:   *K2, M1*
Rnd 6:   *K3, M1*
Rnd 8:   *K4, M1*
Rnd 10:   *K5, M1*
Rnd 12:   *K6,M1*
Rnd 14:   *K7, M1*
Rnd 16:   *K8, M1*
Rnd 18:   *K9, M1*
Rnd 20:   *K10, M1*
Rnd 22:   *K11, M1*
Rnd 24:   *K12, M1*
Rnd 26:   *K13, M1*

Beginning with Rnd 27, K all rnds until the bag measures 20 inches from Rnd 27 (approximately 60 more rnds).

Fur Trim:

When the side of the bag measures 20" from Rnd 27, cut MC, attach 1 strand of the Color B, one strand of Color C, and one strand of Color D. Hold all three together, K 9 rnds. BO.

Finishing:

Felt the bag using your preferred felting method, and shape to dry. Install 8 grommets evenly spaced around the top of the bag, approximately 1" below the bottom of the fur trim.

I-cord Drawcord:

With the size #7 double pointed needles, CO 4 sts using Color E and knit 40" of I-cord. BO. Thread the cord through the 8 grommets before sewing on pom-poms. Make two pom-poms from Color B and attach one to each end of the drawcord.

Opposite where the cord will tie, sew on the purse hooks several inches apart, one above the other to anchor the ends of the shoulder strap. Twist the two drapery tie-backs together and attach to the hooks.

Felting Tutorial, Tips, and Tricks

There are many ways to felt (or more properly termed – full) objects you have knitted. They range from extremely complicated and fussy to very simple. It can be done by hand or by using a washing machine. Given a choice, I'll always opt for simple. I'll describe below the process I always use for felting.

The felting process relies on a combination of physical manipulations of the wool. First, there needs to be strong agitation of the item against some other object. Second, alternating hot water and cold water during the agitation process promotes better shrinkage as the agitation causes the fibers to mat and bind together.

My preference for fabric texture is one that is very dense and thick. To get that texture, I like to felt my objects until the stitch definition is virtually invisible. My process is simple and takes only a few steps --

1. Place the item in a zippered pillow case.
2. Toss it in the washing machine.
3. Add a pair of jeans and one old bath towel.
4. Set the water temperature to hot wash/cold rinse.
5. Set the water fill level to the lowest possible setting.
6. Set the cycle to the normal wash cycle, with no addition of soap or fabric softener.
7. Turn on the machine and when the cycle completes (including spin dry) remove the item and shape to dry.

It couldn't be easier!

The next most important step in getting the look you want is to be meticulous in the shaping process. The shape you create during the knitting process is crucial, and just as important is the shape you create during the drying process. A quick look around your home will reveal several items you can use to mold your felted items as they dry -- a cookie tin, a large book which you can wrap in a plastic bag, a bowl. For items that are relatively flat, a blocking board and blocking pins can be invaluable tools. Items like felted flowers and I-cords can be pinned out on a blocking board and coaxed into perfect shapes.

A few miscellaneous tips to keep in mind —

1. If you have exceptionally hard water, a tablespoon or so of laundry soap or fabric softener in the wash cycle will help the felting process along.
2. Top loading washing machines provide more agitation than front loading machines. Front loaders may require more than one cycle to achieve the best result.
3. Safety pin the zipper pull to the pillow case to keep it from unzipping during the cycle. The pillow case keeps wool lint out of your sewage disposal lines, and also keeps towel lint from working its way into your felted object.
4. Synthetic yarns and cotton will not felt. Only natural animal fibers will felt, and then some will felt better than others.
5. Non-feltable yarns should be used sparingly in felted items so they do not prevent successful felting. When carried along with a strand of wool, they will usually work well.
6. The higher the wool content of a yarn, the better it will felt.
7. Stockinette stitch shrinks more vertically than it does horizontally. My results show that an item knitted in stockinette stitch will shrink about 40% vertically and about 25% horizontally.
8. Garter stitch shrinks differently from stockinette stitch, shrinking about 30% vertically and about 20% horizontally in my experience.

A few words about yarn choice are in order at this point. Choose your yarns carefully! You'll notice that my designs are exclusively knit with yarns from Crystal Palace Yarns. I find them to be the best yarns on the market for felting. They are soft and easy to work with during knitting, and they respond to the felting process with perfect results. Consistent use of these yarns has given me the ability to predict within fractions of an inch what sort of dimensions I'll get from my finished object. I encourage you to knit these designs with their yarns as well and enjoy the plush feeling of the bags when you are done. The felted fabric is soft, dense, luxurious, and wears like iron. There is a wide range of color selections available to choose for these handbags, as well as an extensive collection of coordinating printed yarns to go along with the solids. Other brands could be substituted, of course, but results may not be as expected and may be less predictable.

You may find it helpful to do a practice item before undertaking a larger design from this book, and so here is the pattern for a mini-bag I designed for Crystal Palace Yarns. You can practice on this bag before going on to bigger and better designs. For more of my free designs and to view the complete selection of Crystal Palace Yarns products, please feel free to visit the Crystal Palace Yarns website at www.straw.com.

Mini-Bag Felted with Iceland
Use for gift giving or as tree ornament

Designed, knit and felted by Terry L. Ross for Crystal Palace Yarns
Great for a small gift bag any time of the year or a Christmas tree ornament; this project can be knit in about 2 hours or less.

Terry says, "Each bag uses approximately 50 grams of Crystal Palace Iceland Yarn, so two of the bags in a solid color can be knit from one ball of Iceland. A ball each of Iceland in Red Cerise and New Snow should result in four bags of various color arrangements. Mix and match the yarns to customize the bags in the colors you like. Don't limit yourself to Christmas colors, though . . . this little gift bag will be handy all year long to hold small gifts of all kinds, and can be embellished in many ways to dress it up for the occasion. Hang them on the Christmas tree filled with small trinkets, gift cards, candies, Advent gifts, or other secret treasures, or use empty as tree ornaments as well."

Materials – (2 balls make 4 bags)
Crystal Palace Iceland (100 grams per ball) in your choice of colors, at least one of each color. The bag shown is in #1058 "new snow" & #008 "red cerise"
Crystal Palace Bamboo or DAISY Needles size 11 - 16" circular needle
and 2 US size 11 double point needles (DPNs are for making I-cord)
Stitch Markers (1 regular and 4 split ring)
Tapestry needle
Optional - button or pin to trim the front. (The button here is one Terry made)

Gauge –
3 stitches per inch and 3½ rows per inch in stockinette stitch in the round (don't worry if your gauge is not exact, gauge is not crucial)

Dimensions –
4½" wide, 7" tall, and 2¼" deep before felting, excluding handles.
4" wide, 4" tall, and 2" deep after felting, excluding handles.

Basic instructions for a solid colored bag:

Knit the bottom of the bag –
With the circular needle and your main color, cast on 12 stitches and work 12 rows of garter stitch.

Pick up stitches for the body of the bag –
Continuing around the short edge of the bottom rectangle, pick up 6 stitches on the first short edge, 12 stitches on the next long side, and 6 stitches on the second short edge, then place a stitch marker to designate the beginning of the round. There should be 36 stitches on the needle.
Begin knitting in the round, and knit 25 rounds in stockinette stitch. Bind off all stitches.

I-cord handles –
With the double point needles, cast on 3 stitches and work I-cord until it measures approximately 8½". Leave tails on each end of the cords long enough to stitch them securely to the top of the bag.
Make two cords.

Place the split ring markers at the points on the front and back of the top of the bag where you want to sew on the cord handles, making sure that the fronts and the backs match. Sew on each cord with its attached tails.

Finishing –
Weave in all ends and felt the bag using your preferred method. Shape the bag to dry so that it has the shape of a tiny shopping bag. Embellish as you like with buttons, ribbon, fabric paint, glitter glue, embroidery, felted ornamentation, or whatever else comes to mind.

Ideas for changing up the look of the bag:
For the red and white bag pictured, knit 20 rounds in stockinette stitch with your choice of main color. After 20 rounds, change to a contrast color and knit 5 more rounds. Bind off all stitches. Match I-cord to contrast color.

For a striped bag, knit 2 rounds in one color, then switch to another color and knit 2 rounds. Use as many or as few colors as you like. End the bag with 3 rounds of the last color (for a total of 25 rounds) and knit the I-cords in your choice of coordinating color.

For wider stripes, knit 5 rounds in one color, then switch to another color for 5 rounds, continuing with the striping pattern for a total of 25 rounds. Bind off and knit coordinating I-cords.
Get adventurous and
knit a mixture of various width stripes in a 3 / 2 / 1 / 2 / 3 / 2 / 1 / 2 / 3 / 2 / 1 / 3 round pattern (total 25 rounds).

Carry along a strand of novelty yarn like Crystal Palace Fizz, Popcorn, BeBop, Fizz Stardust, Little Flowers, Squiggle, or Tingle for the last 3 rounds of the bag to give it some texture and pizzazz.

Information and Errata

Every attempt is made to ensure there are no typographical errors or design flaws in the patterns contained herein. However, we recognize that the occasional error may occur. For up to date information about new designs, errata, and other general information, please visit our website at www.terryrossdesigns.com .

About the Designer

Terry Ross is a native Kentuckian who has lived in northern Michigan since late 1989. She and her husband, Art, are the parents of three young children, and though they were blessed with parenthood later in life than most, they find it's helping to forestall the ravages of time.

Terry learned to knit when she was 8 years old by picking up some needles, some yarn, and a little green how-to book from Coats and Clark. Having learned the basics, she put down the needles for 40 years. In 2005, a friend urged her to take it up in earnest, and after some coaxing, she did. Terry managed to finally create an actual knitted object for the first time in her life. She was smitten by knittin'!

Since then, she's prolifically turned out project after project, but found her true love and high calling in the form of knitting and then felting her creations, particularly handbags. She's designed many items for Crystal Palace Yarns which can be downloaded as free patterns and she continues to come up with even more ideas for more felted goods.

Terry's outlook about knitting is that it should be simple to do, while providing attractive style and functionality. She loves to take simple shapes and enhance them with beautiful embellishments, and finds inspiration for designs just about everywhere she looks.

She looks forward to continuing to fan the flames of handbag love with her classic designs.

Knitting Notes

Knitting Notes